I0410756

U.S. HUMANITARIAN ASSISTANCE TO SYRIA: MINIMIZING RISKS AND IMPROVING OVERSIGHT

HEARING

BEFORE THE

SUBCOMMITTEE ON
THE MIDDLE EAST AND NORTH AFRICA

OF THE

COMMITTEE ON FOREIGN AFFAIRS
HOUSE OF REPRESENTATIVES

ONE HUNDRED FOURTEENTH CONGRESS

SECOND SESSION

JULY 14, 2016

Serial No. 114–195

Printed for the use of the Committee on Foreign Affairs

Available via the World Wide Web: http://www.foreignaffairs.house.gov/ or
http://www.gpo.gov/fdsys/

U.S. GOVERNMENT PUBLISHING OFFICE

20–748PDF   WASHINGTON : 2016

For sale by the Superintendent of Documents, U.S. Government Publishing Office
Internet: bookstore.gpo.gov   Phone: toll free (866) 512–1800; DC area (202) 512–1800
Fax: (202) 512–2104   Mail: Stop IDCC, Washington, DC 20402–0001

COMMITTEE ON FOREIGN AFFAIRS

EDWARD R. ROYCE, California, *Chairman*

CHRISTOPHER H. SMITH, New Jersey
ILEANA ROS-LEHTINEN, Florida
DANA ROHRABACHER, California
STEVE CHABOT, Ohio
JOE WILSON, South Carolina
MICHAEL T. McCAUL, Texas
TED POE, Texas
MATT SALMON, Arizona
DARRELL E. ISSA, California
TOM MARINO, Pennsylvania
JEFF DUNCAN, South Carolina
MO BROOKS, Alabama
PAUL COOK, California
RANDY K. WEBER SR., Texas
SCOTT PERRY, Pennsylvania
RON DeSANTIS, Florida
MARK MEADOWS, North Carolina
TED S. YOHO, Florida
CURT CLAWSON, Florida
SCOTT DesJARLAIS, Tennessee
REID J. RIBBLE, Wisconsin
DAVID A. TROTT, Michigan
LEE M. ZELDIN, New York
DANIEL DONOVAN, New York

ELIOT L. ENGEL, New York
BRAD SHERMAN, California
GREGORY W. MEEKS, New York
ALBIO SIRES, New Jersey
GERALD E. CONNOLLY, Virginia
THEODORE E. DEUTCH, Florida
BRIAN HIGGINS, New York
KAREN BASS, California
WILLIAM KEATING, Massachusetts
DAVID CICILLINE, Rhode Island
ALAN GRAYSON, Florida
AMI BERA, California
ALAN S. LOWENTHAL, California
GRACE MENG, New York
LOIS FRANKEL, Florida
TULSI GABBARD, Hawaii
JOAQUIN CASTRO, Texas
ROBIN L. KELLY, Illinois
BRENDAN F. BOYLE, Pennsylvania

AMY PORTER, *Chief of Staff*   THOMAS SHEEHY, *Staff Director*
JASON STEINBAUM, *Democratic Staff Director*

————

SUBCOMMITTEE ON THE MIDDLE EAST AND NORTH AFRICA

ILEANA ROS-LEHTINEN, Florida, *Chairman*

STEVE CHABOT, Ohio
JOE WILSON, South Carolina
DARRELL E. ISSA, California
RANDY K. WEBER SR., Texas
RON DeSANTIS, Florida
MARK MEADOWS, North Carolina
TED S. YOHO, Florida
CURT CLAWSON, Florida
DAVID A. TROTT, Michigan
LEE M. ZELDIN, New York

THEODORE E. DEUTCH, Florida
GERALD E. CONNOLLY, Virginia
BRIAN HIGGINS, New York
DAVID CICILLINE, Rhode Island
ALAN GRAYSON, Florida
GRACE MENG, New York
LOIS FRANKEL, Florida
BRENDAN F. BOYLE, Pennsylvania

CONTENTS

U.S. HUMANITARIAN ASSISTANCE TO SYRIA: MINIMIZING RISKS AND IMPROVING OVERSIGHT

THURSDAY, JULY 14, 2016

House of Representatives,
Subcommittee on the Middle East and North Africa,
Committee on Foreign Affairs,
Washington, DC.

The subcommittee met, pursuant to notice, at 2:19 p.m., in room 2172, Rayburn House Office Building, Hon. Ileana Ros-Lehtinen (chairman of the subcommittee) presiding.

Ms. Ros-Lehtinen. The subcommittee will come to order.

I know that Mr. Deutch is right in the side room, so he will be right out. And my apologies for starting late.

After recognizing myself and Ranking Member Deutch for 5 minutes each for opening statements, I will then recognize other members seeking recognition for 1 minute. We will then hear from our witnesses.

And without objection, the witnesses' prepared statements will be made a part of the record. Apologies for keeping you waiting.

And members may have 5 days to insert statements and questions for the record, subject to the length limitation in the rules.

I would first like to thank all of the individuals and organizations involved in providing humanitarian assistance for the Syrian crisis. Working in an active conflict zone is incredibly dangerous but also desperately needed. So we thank you and we support you.

Today's hearing is the subcommittee's fourth hearing that focuses specifically on the Syrian humanitarian crisis. It has been an issue we have been following closely since the fighting in Syria began over 5 years ago. And until the administration gets serious about developing a comprehensive plan to end the conflict, it will, unfortunately, be an issue we will continue to revisit.

The numbers are truly staggering. By most estimates, there have been at least ¼ million Syrians killed and possibly as much as nearly ½ million. Nearly 5 million Syrians have fled to neighboring countries like Turkey, Lebanon, and Jordan. There are nearly 7 million internally displaced Syrians and more than 13½ million people are in need of assistance, with about 5½ million people in besieged and hard-to-reach areas.

We have convened this hearing today to see how we can maximize our efforts and limit risks when providing humanitarian assistance.

In addition to the $5 billion already provided, Secretary Kerry announced, earlier this week, $439 million in additional humanitarian assistance, and the President's budget request for Fiscal Year 2017 seeks nearly $2.1 billion through accounts that addresses the humanitarian impact of this crisis.

This is a lot to ask of the U.S. taxpayers, especially when we know that there is no end in sight to this terrible crisis. And that is why Congress must conduct oversight, to ensure that this assistance is being used as effectively and efficiently as possible. And that is why I was pleased to be joined by Ranking Member Deutch, Gerry Connolly, and Ron DeSantis in requesting a GAO review of our Syrian humanitarian assistance program.

This report focuses solely on our programs inside Syria. With the U.S. no longer having a presence in the country, we have to rely on remote programs and coordinating with implementing partners. We recognize this brings challenges, but these challenges also make it more important for our agencies to mitigate all risks, because situations like these make our effort more vulnerable to waste, fraud, abuse, and diversion. And that is precisely what GAO and USAID's Inspector General have found, that we have weaknesses in our humanitarian aid programs in Syria and both State and USAID could improve their fraud oversight.

GAO's review found that most of the implementing partners that we work with to provide humanitarian assistance into Syria do not assess the risk of fraud. Why is this important? Well, we will hear from the Inspector General that her office has opened 25 cases to investigate allegations of abuse of USAID funds with three common fraud schemes. This, obviously, raises concerns, not only with how USAID and State oversee our assistance programs, but it raises concerns regarding the checks and balances our implementing partners have in place as well.

We rely heavily on our partners, as does the U.N., where 75 percent of all our assistance is funneled through. And if they are lax in their oversight, we run the risk of wider loss due to waste, fraud, and abuse, and diversion.

What GAO also found is that not only do most implementing partners not assess the risk of fraud, but their controls for mitigating the risk of fraud and loss were not informed by a risk assessment. So it is likely that they either don't know what they are looking for or are looking in the wrong place. And that is why GAO has recommended that USAID and State strengthen their fraud oversight themselves, but they must also require implementing partners to conduct fraud risk assessment and to ensure monitors are properly trained. These are common sense recommendations for our efforts in Syria, but they are also common sense for State and USAID across the board.

We provide large sums of money and assistance every year and administer very large programs. We need to be doing everything we can to minimize the risk of waste, fraud, abuse, and diversion. It is also important because we do send most of our assistance through the U.N., and from there we have less oversight, less transparency. If we can work with our implementing partners to strengthen how they assess the risk of fraud and how they improve their oversight, we have a better chance of maximizing the humanitarian assistance response across the board.

State and USAID are doing a good job with their humanitarian response, but we can always seek to do better. We all want to ensure that we are being proper stewards of American taxpayer dollars, but we are also promoting our core ideals and values as Americans by doing what we can to help those suffering from the ongoing crisis in Syria. So I am eager to hear from our witnesses on how we can accomplish both of these objectives without sacrificing our ability to assist those in dire need.

And with that, I apologize to our ranking member for my lateness, and he is recognized.

Mr. DEUTCH. Thank you, Madam Chairman. It was an honor to arrive before you——

Ms. ROS-LEHTINEN. Thank you.

Mr. DEUTCH [continuing]. Once. First time ever.

Thanks so much for holding today's hearing, and thanks for your continued commitment to making sure that this committee keeps the humanitarian response to this herein crisis at the forefront of our work.

And thank you to Congressman Connolly and Congressman DeSantis for joining us in requesting the GAO report to review our humanitarian assistance to Syria. Because of the extent of U.S. commitment to responding to this humanitarian crisis, this report is not only very timely, but it is extremely important for the safety and for the accountability of our aid programs.

I also thank our witnesses for appearing here today and for the work that you do to ensure proper oversight of aid to the Syrian people who are in critical need.

The humanitarian crisis in Syria has reached staggering heights. I repeat these figures at every hearing because we have to take a moment to just try to grasp the magnitude of the crisis. There are now more than 13½ million people inside Syria in need of immediate humanitarian assistance. 13½ million people of which 6½ million are internally displaced. These people require health care, water and sanitation, shelter, food, and all of them desperately need protection. Since the crisis began in 2011, Syria's development situation has regressed almost by four decades, and the life expectancy among Syrians has dropped more than 20 years.

This humanitarian catastrophe is exacerbated further by the Assad regime, which has intentionally obstructed access to the Syrian people. The regime leverages food and water as a weapon of war. The regime's systematic denial of medical assistance, food supplies, and other humanitarian aid to people living in besieged areas is unacceptable. It is illegal under international law.

There are over 5 million people in hard-to-reach areas, including close to 600,000 people in 18 besieged areas who are dying from starvation. This flagrant violation of international humanitarian norms must end. The number of deaths surpasses 400,000 Syrians, and this number increases every day. These are not just numbers; they are human lives, and we must continue to think of that.

I commend the hundreds of aid workers, NGOs, and implementing partners that are on the ground risking their lives to provide food and medical care to the Syrian people. They, you, are doing an exceptional job in extraordinarily difficult circumstances, and I don't think that you get the credit that you deserve.

I am proud that the United States has stepped up to lead the worldwide humanitarian response effort. The U.S. has consistently led global funding efforts since 2013, and our total funding has passed $5 billion at the end of this year. Other donor countries must now fulfill their pledges, something that we say at every one of these hearings, and it continues to be true and urgent. Yet the scale of the need continues to grow.

I understand that the humanitarian response of this size is not easy, especially in an operating environment that is particularly dangerous and hostile. Delivery of U.S. humanitarian assistance inside Syria is further complicated by a reliance on partners who can deliver cross-border aid. This means USAID and other international NGOs have been forced to oversee assistance remotely from neighboring countries, including Turkey and Jordan.

USAID has relied on implementing partners to cross the border into Syria to deliver assistance into both government and opposition controlled areas. These cross-border operations only increase the opportunity for risks and fraud and for other entities and individuals to take advantage of our resources. This is troubling.

When I hear about organized criminal networks infiltrating aid organizations or instances of bribery, bid rigging, delivery of products of lower quality, or even the failure of delivery altogether, I am concerned about where the gaps exist within our humanitarian assistance programs. I am concerned whether these programs have adequately assessed the risks and provided the necessary oversight of the programs and their partners. Our aid agency and partners need to be prepared for potential risk and fraud, especially in a context like this. They need to consistently review and verify that they are meeting financial obligations and holding the highest standards for aid products and partners.

The GAO found that although USAID had guidelines for verifying the progress of activities in Syria, they did not include clear instructions to identify and recognize potential fraud risks. Moreover, field monitors did not receive fraud awareness training.

When internal controls monitoring and financial oversight plans fail, it puts taxpayer dollars at risk. But more importantly, it delays the critical and crucial assistance to those who are depending on this aid. It diverts resources from those who need it most. We need to keep our agencies and partners accountable. The Syrian people deserve that, and I am pleased to see that USAID has concurred and is in the process of implementing all of the GAO recommendations. I am also pleased that USAID has increased its own third-party monitoring of programs.

It is a war zone out there. We understand there will be unforeseen circumstances and challenges. There will, unfortunately, always be situations where individuals will attempt to take advantage of the chaos. Despite all these challenges, we need to have that confidence that the agencies are doing all they possibly can to mitigate fraud and mismanagement of our resources. We need to have the confidence that the agencies have made all the necessary risk assessments and are continually monitoring and updating procedures to close the gaps and vulnerabilities.

I applaud USAID for working so quickly to address these gaps, and I am hopeful that the measures that the USAID has put in place as a result of both the GAO and OIG's work will give us that confidence. All of that is to say, while there are many obstacles to assisting Syrians, we are helping millions and we are saving many, many lives. Americans can be proud that we are the largest donor country to the Syrian crisis, that we have the largest donor world-wide to humanitarian assistance. We are committed to living up to our values and to meeting the needs of the millions in crisis.

I look to our witnesses today to help us better understand the situation on the ground and to their recommendations.

And, Madam Chairman, before I yield back, I would take just a moment of personal privilege, if I may. Julie Ahn, who is sitting behind me, is a Rangel Fellow from the State Department, who is completing her internship with us before she heads off to the Kennedy School in the fall. She will then be entering the foreign service to pursue the good work that our foreign service officers do all around the world.

Ms. Ros-Lehtinen. Yeah. Two lovely years in Kurdistan.

Mr. Deutch. So I thank you very much and I appreciate your giving me that opportunity.

I yield back.

Ms. Ros-Lehtinen. Thank you.

So safe speed and may all go well.

And now, I would like to turn for any opening statements that they would like to make to Randy Weber of Texas and then to be followed by Ron DeSantis of Florida.

Mr. Weber. I am good and I am ready to go. Thank you.

Ms. Ros-Lehtinen. Texans are always ready.

Ron?

Mr. DeSantis. Let's get this show on the road.

Ms. Ros-Lehtinen. Let's do it.

Well, thank you. And I know Lee Zeldin is there on the side, and if he comes back, we will recognize him.

But the subcommittee is delighted to welcome back Dr. Thomas Melito, who serves as the director of the International Affairs and Trade team at the Government Accountability Office, GAO. In this capacity, Dr. Melito is primarily responsible for GAO's multilateral assistance portfolio as well as other areas of important oversight.

So welcome back.

And next, we would like to welcome to our subcommittee for the first time, but we know that it is going to be a repeated engagement, Ms. Ann Calvaresi Barr, who serves as the Inspector General for the United States Agency of International Development, USAID. In this capacity, she leads the USAID Office of Inspector General exercising broad oversight authority over programs and operations of USAID, as well as the Millennium Challenge Corporation, the U.S. African Development Foundation, the Inter-American Foundation, and the Overseas Private Investment Corporation. They sure keep you busy.

So it is my understanding that the two of you came through GAO at the same time, so this is a very public reunion of sorts. We welcome you. Welcome, both of you.

And we will start with Dr. Melito.

**STATEMENT OF MR. THOMAS MELITO, DIRECTOR, INTER-
NATIONAL AFFAIRS AND TRADE, GOVERNMENT ACCOUNT-
ABILITY OFFICE**

Mr. MELITO. Madam Chairman, Ranking Member Deutch, and
members of the subcommittee, I am pleased to be here to discuss
the work you requested on delivery of U.S. humanitarian assistance——

Ms. ROS-LEHTINEN. If you could bring that microphone a little bit
closer.

Mr. MELITO. I am pleased to be here to discuss the work you requested on delivery of U.S. humanitarian assistance to people inside Syria. The conflict in Syria has created a complex humanitarian challenge. As of May 2016, the U.N. reported that 13½ million people inside Syria have been affected by the conflict and are
in need of humanitarian assistance such as food, shelter, and medicine.

Since the start of the conflict in March 2011, the United States,
through the Department of State and USAID, has provided over $5
billion in humanitarian assistance, about half of which has been
provided for assistance to people inside Syria. In 2015, the U.S.
provided more than a quarter of the total international funding for
the humanitarian response to Syria.

My testimony summarizes our report on the delivery of U.S. humanitarian assistance to people inside Syria, which is being released today. I will focus on four topics. First, factors affecting delivery of assistance. Second, the extent to which State, USAID, and
their partners have assessed risks to their program. Third, implementation of controls to mitigate identifying risks and ensure appropriate financial oversight of humanitarian assistance projects.
And fourth, GAO's recommendations and the agency responses.

Regarding the first topic, several factors complicate the delivery
of humanitarian assistance to people inside Syria. For example, the
increasingly violent and widespread Syrian conflict has hindered
effective delivery of humanitarian assistance. In addition, administrative procedures put in place by the Syrian Government have delayed or limited the delivery of humanitarian assistance, especially
to besieged areas. Further, due to restrictions for traveling to
Syria, State and USAID staff must manage the delivery of humanitarian assistance remotely from neighboring countries.

Regarding the second topic on risk assessments, U.S. agencies do
not require comprehensive risk assessments from implementing
partners, and most partners have not assessed the risk of fraud.
Risk assessment involves comprehensively identifying risks associated with achieving program objectives and determining actions to
mitigate those risks. In the context of Syria, such risks include
theft, fraud, and safety and security.

Most of the implementing partners we examined conducted formal risk assessments for at least one type of risk, most commonly
security risk. In addition, several maintain assessments on a variety of risks that are updated on a regular basis. However, few of
these implementing partners conducted risk assessments for the
risk of fraud, despite elevated risks for fraud in assistance projects
inside Syria. These risks have been highlighted through the ongoing and closed fraud investigations by USAID's Inspector General.

Absent assessments of fraud risk, implementing partners may not have all the information needed to design appropriate controls to mitigate such risk. In addition, State and USAID officials may not have sufficient awareness of the risk of fraud or loss due to theft.

Regarding the third topic on oversight, partners have implemented controls to mitigate some of the risks of delivering humanitarian assistance inside Syria, but U.S. agencies could improve their oversight of these programs. We found that partners we examined had implemented controls to mitigate certain risks of delivering humanitarian assistance inside Syria. For example, many partners implemented controls to account for safety and security risks to their personnel and beneficiaries receiving assistance. However, we found that fraud oversight could be strengthened.

While USAID has hired a contractor for verifying the progress of activities in Syria, they have not clearly instructed field monitors on how to identify and collect information on potential fraud risks. Further, the contractors have not received fraud awareness training.

Regarding the fourth topic, GAO made several recommendations in our report. To provide more complete information to assist the agencies in conducting oversight activities, State and USAID should require the implementing partners to conduct fraud risk assessments. In addition, USAID should ensure its field monitors are trained to identify potential fraud risks and collect information on them. Both agencies agreed with GAO's recommendations.

Madam Chairman, Ranking Member Deutch, and members of the subcommittee, this completes my prepared statement. I will be pleased to respond to any questions you may have at this time.

[The prepared statement of Mr. Melito follows:]

United States Government Accountability Office

Testimony

Before the Subcommittee on the Middle East and North Africa, Committee on Foreign Affairs, House of Representatives

For Release on Delivery
Expected at 2:00 p.m ET
Thursday, July 14, 2016

SYRIA HUMANITARIAN ASSISTANCE

Implementing Partners Have Assessed Some Risks of Providing Aid inside Syria, but U.S. Agencies Could Improve Fraud Oversight

Statement of Thomas Melito, Director, International Affairs and Trade

GAO-16-808T

Chairman Ros-Lehtinen, Ranking Member Deutch, and Members of the Subcommittee:

Thank you for the opportunity to discuss our work on the delivery of U.S. humanitarian assistance to people inside Syria. The conflict in Syria has created a complex humanitarian challenge. As of May 2016, the United Nations (UN) reported that 13.5 million people inside Syria have been affected by the conflict and are in need of humanitarian assistance, such as food, shelter, and medicine. Since the start of the conflict in March 2011, the United States, through the Department of State (State) and the U.S. Agency for International Development (USAID), has provided over $5 billion in humanitarian assistance, about half of which has been provided for assistance to people inside Syria. USAID provides funds to UN organizations and also works through nongovernmental organizations (NGO) inside Syria, while State works through three main partners—two UN organizations and one public international organization. U.S. humanitarian assistance is part of a broader international response. Since 2013, the United States has consistently led global funding efforts—for example, the United States provided more than a quarter of the total international funding for the 2015 Syria humanitarian response.

My testimony summarizes our 2016 report on the delivery of U.S. humanitarian assistance to people inside Syria, which is being released today.[1] In this report, we examine humanitarian assistance provided by State, USAID, and their implementing partners to people inside Syria, including (1) factors affecting delivery of such assistance; (2) the extent to which State, USAID, and their partners have assessed risks to the programs; and (3) implementation of controls to mitigate identified risks and ensure appropriate financial oversight of humanitarian assistance projects. To determine factors affecting delivery of assistance, we conducted a content analysis of monthly United Nations Secretary General (UNSG) reports on the humanitarian situation in Syria to categorize and summarize observations contained in the reports. We also interviewed cognizant officials. To determine the extent to which State, USAID, and their partners have assessed risks to the programs, and to evaluate implementation of controls to mitigate risks and ensure

---

[1] GAO, *Syria Humanitarian Assistance: Some Risks of Providing Aid inside Syria Assessed, but U.S. Agencies Could Improve Fraud Oversight*, GAO-16-829 (Washington, D.C., July 14, 2016).

appropriate financial oversight of assistance, we selected a nongeneralizable sample of 12 of 52 fiscal year 2015 State and USAID funding instruments[2] from 9 different implementing partners and evaluated the risk assessments and control activities associated with the funding instruments.

Our review resulted in the following findings. First, several factors complicate the delivery of humanitarian assistance to people inside Syria. Second, U.S. agencies and implementing partners have assessed some risks of delivering humanitarian assistance inside Syria, but most partners have not assessed risks of fraud. Lastly, partners have implemented controls to mitigate certain risks of delivering humanitarian assistance inside Syria, but U.S. agencies could improve their oversight of these programs. As a result, we made several recommendations to State and USAID to improve financial oversight.

Several Factors Affect the Delivery of Humanitarian Assistance to People inside Syria

We identified three key factors that affect delivery of humanitarian assistance to people inside Syria. First, the increasingly violent and widespread Syrian conflict has hindered effective delivery of humanitarian assistance. Based on our analysis of monthly UNSG reports on the situation inside Syria, as well as interviews with officials providing assistance to Syria based both inside and outside of the country, humanitarian assistance is routinely prevented or delayed from reaching its intended target due to shifting conflict lines, attacks on aid facilities and workers, an inability to access besieged areas, and other factors related to active conflict (see fig. 1).

---

[2]For the purposes of this report, we use the term "funding instrument" to refer to assistance instruments that are used to transfer money, property, or services to accomplish a public purpose. Grants, cooperative agreements, and voluntary contributions are all types of funding instruments that the U.S. government uses to provide humanitarian assistance to people inside Syria.

Figure 1: Damage to Health Facilities in Syria after Aerial Attack, Tel Shehab, Dara'a Province (left) and Al Khaf, Rural Damascus (right)

Source: USAID Office of U.S. Foreign Disaster Assistance (OFDA) implementing partner. | GAO-16-808T

Second, administrative procedures put in place by the Syrian government have delayed or limited the delivery of humanitarian assistance, according to UNSG reports. These reports detail multiple instances of unanswered requests for approvals of convoys, denial or removal of medical supplies from convoys, difficulty obtaining visas for humanitarian staff, and restrictions on international and national NGOs' ability to operate. As of May 2016, the UNSG reported that 4.6 million people inside Syria are located in hard-to-reach areas and more than 500,000 of those remain besieged by Islamic State of Iraq and Syria, the government of Syria, or non-State armed opposition groups. The UN further reported that in 2015, only 10 percent of all requests for UN interagency convoys to hard-to-reach and besieged areas were approved and assistance delivered. In addition, according to implementing partner officials based in Damascus, Syria, even when these convoys were approved, the officials participating in delivering the assistance were subjected to hours-long delays.

Third, due to restrictions, USAID and State staff manage the delivery of humanitarian assistance in Syria remotely from neighboring countries. The U.S. government closed its embassy in Damascus, Syria, in 2012 due to security conditions and the safety of personnel, among other factors. In the absence of direct program monitoring, USAID and State officials noted that they utilize information provided by implementing partners to help ensure effective delivery of assistance and to help their financial oversight, including mitigating risks such as fraud, theft, diversion, and loss. However, USAID officials in the region explained to us that while partners provide data and information, their inability to consistently access project sites—due to factors such as ongoing fighting, bombing raids, and border closures—limited the extent to which partners could obtain and verify progress. Past audit work has shown challenges to such an approach, including cases of partners not fully implementing monitoring practices, resulting in limited project accountability. Further, USAID Office of Inspector General (OIG) has reported that aid organizations providing life-saving assistance in Syria and the surrounding region face an extremely high-risk environment, and that the absence of adequate internal controls, among other challenges, can jeopardize the integrity of these relief efforts and deny critical aid to those in need.

U.S. Agencies and Their Implementing Partners Have Assessed Some Risks to Their Programs, but Most Partners Have Not Assessed Fraud Risks

State, USAID, and their implementing partners have assessed some types of risk to their programs inside Syria, but most partners have not assessed the risk of fraud. Risk assessment involves comprehensively identifying risks associated with achieving program objectives; analyzing those risks to determine their significance, likelihood of occurrence, and impact; and determining actions or controls to mitigate the risk. In the context of Syria, such risks could include theft and diversion; fraud; safety; security; program governance; and implementing partner capacity risks.

Most of the implementing partners in our sample have conducted formal risk assessments for at least one type of risk, especially security risk, and several maintain risk registers that assess a wide variety of risks (see table 1). However, few implementing partners have conducted risk assessments for the risk of fraud (four of nine), or for the risk of loss due to theft or diversion (four of nine). According to GAO's *A Framework for Managing Fraud Risks in Federal Programs*,[3] effective fraud risk

---

[3]GAO, *A Framework for Managing Fraud Risks in Federal Programs*, GAO-15-593SP (Washington, D.C.: July 2015).

management involves fully considering the specific fraud risks the agency or program faces, analyzing the potential likelihood and impact of fraud schemes, and prioritizing fraud risks. In addition, risk assessment is essential for ensuring that partners design appropriate and effective control activities. Control activities to mitigate the risk of fraud should be directly connected to the fraud risk assessments and, over time, managers may adjust the control activities if they determine that controls are not effectively designed or implemented to reduce the likelihood or impact of an inherent fraud risk to a tolerable risk level.

Table 1: Selected Risks Identified in Risk Assessments Conducted by Implementing Partners in Our Sample

Risk	Vulnerability	Number of implementing partners out of a total of 9 who conducted assessments for this type of risk
Safety of personnel	Road accidents, road banditry, and ambushes while driving are all safety risks for implementing partner personnel	7
Security environment	Gathering of large crowds for distribution of humanitarian assistance can cause security risks for beneficiaries	8
Loss due to theft or diversion	Diversion of humanitarian aid by armed groups or criminal elements	4
Fraud	Remote management of programs can weaken internal controls and increase opportunities for fraud and waste	4

Source: GAO analysis of implementing partner documents. | GAO-16-808T

Although most of the implementing partners in our sample did not conduct assessments of the risk of fraud, there are elevated risks for fraud in U.S. funded humanitarian assistance projects for people inside Syria. According to officials at USAID OIG, they have four ongoing investigations of allegations of fraud and mismanagement related to programs for delivering humanitarian assistance to people inside Syria. Two of the investigations involve allegations of procurement fraud, bribery, and product substitution in USAID funded humanitarian cross-border programs related to procurements of non-food items. One of these investigations found that the subawardee of the implementing partner failed to distribute nonfood items in southern Syria, instead subcontracting the distribution to another organization, but nevertheless billed USAID for the full cost of the project. Additionally, the subawardee was reliant on one individual to facilitate the transfer of materials and salaries, and this individual was involved in the alteration and falsification of records related to the distribution of the nonfood items. According to the USAID OIG, senior leadership at the subawardee was aware of these facts.[4] Further, in May 2016, USAID OIG reported the identification of bid-rigging and multiple bribery and kickback schemes related to contracts to deliver humanitarian aid in Syria, investigations of which resulted in the suspension of 14 entities and individuals involved with aid programs from Turkey. Without documented risk assessments, implementing partners may not have all of the information needed to design appropriate controls to mitigate fraud risks, and State and USAID may not have visibility into areas of risk, such as fraud and loss due to theft and diversion.

Partners Have Implemented Controls for Delivering Humanitarian Assistance inside Syria, but U.S. Agencies Could Improve Oversight

We found that partners in our sample had implemented controls to mitigate certain risks of delivering humanitarian assistance inside Syria. For instance, many partners in our sample implemented controls to account for safety and security risks to their personnel and beneficiaries receiving assistance. Some partners identified aerial targeting of humanitarian aid workers and beneficiaries at distribution points as a major vulnerability and implemented controls to mitigate this risk, such as distributing goods to beneficiaries on overcast days and making door-to-door deliveries of aid packages. In addition, partners in our sample implemented controls to mitigate risks of fraud and loss within their operations. For example, officials from two implementing partners we interviewed in Amman, Jordan, stated that they conducted spot checks of assistance packages in warehouses to confirm the quantity of the contents and ensure that the quality of the items complied with the terms of the contract. According to another implementing partner, officials from its organization visit the vendor warehouses before signing contracts to verify that U.S. government commodity safety and quality assurance guidelines are met. However, the majority of controls to mitigate risks of fraud and loss were not informed by a risk assessment (see table 2).

---

[4]According to the USAID OIG, as result of OIG's investigative findings, USAID decided to terminate the sub-award and reduce its planned funding to the prime implementer by $10,500,000.

Table 2: Selected Mitigating Control Activities That Responded to Identified Risks

Risk	Vulnerability	Mitigating Activity	Number of implementing partners out of a total of 9 who conducted assessments for this type of risk	Number of implementing partners out of a total of 9 with control activities for this type of risk
Safety of personnel	Road accidents, road banditry, and ambushes while driving are all safety risks for implementing partner personnel	Provide instruction to drivers on methods for taking evasive action and fleeing to safety	7	8
Security environment	Gathering of large crowds for distribution of humanitarian assistance can cause security risks for beneficiaries	Conduct door-to-door distribution—rather than distribution from a centralized location—in high-risk environments	8	9
Loss due to theft or diversion	Diversion of aid by armed groups or criminal elements	Obtain community acceptance through liaising with local councils; track and monitor supplies	4	9
Fraud	Remote management of programs can weaken internal controls and increase opportunities for fraud and waste	Train new staff and existing staff on fraud awareness; triangulate data and information from monitoring in programmatic and financial operations	4	8

Source: GAO analysis of implementing partner documents. | GAO-16-806T

State and USAID have taken steps to oversee partner programs delivering humanitarian assistance inside Syria; nevertheless, opportunities to assess and mitigate the potential impact of fraud risks remain. U.S. officials cited a variety of oversight activities. For instance, State officials in the region conduct quarterly meetings with partners and collect information on programmatic objectives and on partner programs. State also has enhanced monitoring plans in place with its implementing partners to augment quarterly reporting with information on risks of diversion of assistance. Similarly, USAID officials in Washington, D.C., told us they screen proposals from partners to identify risk mitigation activities and USAID officials in the region noted they maintain regular contact with partners, attend monthly meetings with them, conduct random spot-checks of aid packages at warehouse facilities, and coordinate activities among partners to reduce or eliminate duplication or overlap of assistance. Moreover, according to USAID officials, the USAID

OIG has conducted fraud awareness training for officials in the region to improve their ability to detect fraud, such as product substitution, when they conduct spot-checks of aid packages at warehouse facilities. Further, in October 2015, USAID's Office of U.S. Foreign Disaster Assistance hired a third party monitoring organization to review its projects in Syria. By February 2016, field monitors had conducted site visits and submitted monitoring reports to USAID, providing information on the status of projects and including major concerns that field monitors identified.

We found that fraud oversight could be strengthened. Based on our analysis, USAID's third party monitoring contract and supporting documentation contain guidelines for verifying the progress of activities in Syria; however, they do not clearly instruct field monitors to identify potential fraud risks as they conduct site assessments of projects in Syria. Furthermore, the monitoring plan and site visit templates do not contain specific guidance on how to recognize fraud, and field monitors have not received the USAID OIG fraud awareness training, according to USAID officials. Leading practices in fraud risk management suggest evaluating outcomes using a risk-based approach and adapting activities to improve fraud risk management. This includes conducting risk-based monitoring and evaluation of fraud risk management activities with a focus on outcome measurement and using the results to improve prevention, detection, and response.

The monitoring plan associated with the contract contains guidelines for field monitors to document their assessment of the project at the completion of a site visit. However, it lacks specific guidelines to identify potential fraud risks during site visits. Additionally, the templates created by the third party monitoring organization to document site visits instruct monitors to verify the presence or absence of supplies and their quality, among other instructions, but lack specific fraud indicators to alert field monitors to collect information on and identify potential fraud. Furthermore, the monitoring plan contains a training curriculum for field monitors, which has several objectives designed to familiarize them with the protocols, procedures, and instruments used for data collection and reporting. However, the curriculum does not have specific courses for recognizing potential or actual instances of fraud that may occur on site. Given the opportunity for fraud that exists in humanitarian assistance programs, as well as the ongoing USAID OIG investigations, without instructions to specifically collect data on fraud and training to identify it, USAID may be missing an opportunity to assist in its activities to mitigate fraud risks and design appropriate controls.

Our Recommendations and Agency Responses	We made several recommendations in our report. To provide more complete information to assist the agencies in conducting oversight activities, State and USAID should require their implementing partners to conduct fraud risk assessments. In addition, USAID should ensure its field monitors (1) are trained to identify potential fraud risks and (2) collect information on them. State and USAID concurred with our recommendations. Chairman Ros-Lehtinen, Ranking Member Deutch, Members of the Subcommittee, this completes my prepared statement. I would be pleased to respond to any questions that you may have at this time.
GAO Contact and Staff Acknowledgments	For further information about this testimony, please contact Thomas Melito, Director, International Affairs and Trade at (202) 512-9601 or melitot@gao gov. Contact points for our Offices of Congressional Relations and Public Affairs may be found on the last page of this statement. GAO staff who made key contributions to this testimony are Elizabeth Repko (Assistant Director), Jennifer Young, Kyerion Printup, Justine Lazaro, Cristina Norland, Karen Deans, Kimberly McGatlin, Diane Morris, Justin Fisher, and Alex Welsh.

18

GAO's Mission	The Government Accountability Office, the audit, evaluation, and investigative arm of Congress, exists to support Congress in meeting its constitutional responsibilities and to help improve the performance and accountability of the federal government for the American people. GAO examines the use of public funds; evaluates federal programs and policies; and provides analyses, recommendations, and other assistance to help Congress make informed oversight, policy, and funding decisions. GAO's commitment to good government is reflected in its core values of accountability, integrity, and reliability.
Obtaining Copies of GAO Reports and Testimony	The fastest and easiest way to obtain copies of GAO documents at no cost is through GAO's website (http://www.gao.gov). Each weekday afternoon, GAO posts on its website newly released reports, testimony, and correspondence. To have GAO e-mail you a list of newly posted products, go to http://www.gao.gov and select "E-mail Updates."
Order by Phone	The price of each GAO publication reflects GAO's actual cost of production and distribution and depends on the number of pages in the publication and whether the publication is printed in color or black and white. Pricing and ordering information is posted on GAO's website, http://www.gao.gov/ordering.htm. Place orders by calling (202) 512-6000, toll free (866) 801-7077, or TDD (202) 512-2537. Orders may be paid for using American Express, Discover Card, MasterCard, Visa, check, or money order. Call for additional information.
Connect with GAO	Connect with GAO on Facebook, Flickr, Twitter, and YouTube. Subscribe to our RSS Feeds or E-mail Updates. Listen to our Podcasts and read The Watchblog. Visit GAO on the web at www.gao.gov.
To Report Fraud, Waste, and Abuse in Federal Programs	Contact: Website: http://www.gao.gov/fraudnet/fraudnet.htm E-mail: fraudnet@gao.gov Automated answering system: (800) 424-5454 or (202) 512-7470
Congressional Relations	Katherine Siggerud, Managing Director, siggerudk@gao.gov, (202) 512-4400, U.S. Government Accountability Office, 441 G Street NW, Room 7125, Washington, DC 20548
Public Affairs	Chuck Young, Managing Director, youngc1@gao.gov, (202) 512-4800 U.S. Government Accountability Office, 441 G Street NW, Room 7149 Washington, DC 20548

Ms. ROS-LEHTINEN. Thank you very much.
Ms. Calvaresi.

STATEMENT OF THE HONORABLE ANN CALVARESI BARR, IN-SPECTOR GENERAL, OFFICE OF THE INSPECTOR GENERAL, UNITED STATES AGENCY FOR INTERNATIONAL DEVELOP-MENT

Ms. CALVARESI BARR. Madam Chairman, Ranking Member Deutch, and members of the subcommittee, thank you for inviting me to discuss USAID's efforts to provide humanitarian assistance to the more than 13 million in Syria affected by the crisis there. The billions of dollars USAID has invested not only provide relief to those impacted, it strengthens our standing in the world. Yet despite our goodwill, bad characters have taken advantage of the complex situation for personal gain, ultimately denying Syrian people the food, clothing, health care, and other aid they urgently need.

Today, I will summarize the actions our special agents and investigators have taken to uncover and stop fraud. I will also highlight several program management concerns exposed by these investigations.

When the U.S. designated the response to Syria as a contingency operation, we ramped up our oversight in the region. OIG investigators briefed hundreds of USAID and implementer staff on fraud indicators and developed a comprehensive handbook for how to identify and report fraud. They also stood up the Syria Investigations Working Group to share information with other U.S. and international oversight organizations about ongoing investigative issues.

To date, we have received 116 complaints of alleged abuse and have opened 25 investigations. Some complaints relate to terrorist diversions, but the majority, roughly two-thirds, relate to theft and fraud schemes, such as collusion, product substitution, and false claims. For example, vendors paid bribes or kickbacks to implementer staff in exchange for competitive bidding data or manipulation of bid evaluations.

One of our product substitution cases involved a Turkish vendor that placed more salt and less lentils in food kits to increase their profits. We also found nonfood kits in a warehouse in Syria that were missing items or included substandard products, such as poor quality frying pans that can easily be bent and folded and tarps that were too small to shelter an adult. In one false claims case, a Jordanian NGO fabricated documentation that it distributed nonfood items to communities in southern Syria when, in fact, the goods were distributed by another organization at its own expense.

To date, we have made seven referrals to USAID regarding nine implementers. These referrals prompted USAID actions ranging from employee and program suspensions and terminations to now placing specific conditions on implementer awards and agreements. Our investigative outcomes have resulted in $11.5 million in savings and six programmatic suspensions of awards valued at $305 million. This represents about a third of the money USAID disbursed in Fiscal Years 2015 and 2016. This demonstrates the impact our work has had and the proactive measures taken to further prevent losses.

Our investigative cases not only stopped fraud, but also raised a number of concerns about implementer procurement practices and internal controls for managing projects as well as USAID's oversight.

First, we question whether implementers' procurement policies and internal controls are appropriate for the high-risk environment. In an effort to expedite procurements, implementers used an emergency waiver to bypass established procurement policies and procedures, including full and open competition. While the use of these waivers is allowable when the needs are urgent, they were used for an extended period of time and were not accompanied by enhanced monitoring. Internal control concerns relate to implementers' quality control procedures such as allowing vendors to ship materials across the border without the items being inspected and accepting substandard items. In addition, some implementers did not pursue allegations, overlooked evidence of wrongdoing, or did not notify USAID or OIG of internal investigations.

Finally, our cases point to potential gaps in USAID oversight of implementers. For example, OFDA generally did not require implementers to obtain prior agency approval of large subcontracts or set requirements to inspect them. Further, DART teams responsible for coordinating and managing response efforts did not include permanent subject-matter experts to evaluate procured items.

While we are encouraged by the steps USAID has taken and plans to take in response to the vulnerabilities we identified, continued vigilance and a better understanding of program deficiencies is required. To that end, my office, along with our partners at DOD and State, remain committed to aggressively cracking down on fraud, waste, and abuse. Concurrently, my office plans to advance audit work aimed at identifying systemic weaknesses and additional actions USAID can take to eliminating vulnerabilities before they can be further exploited.

Providing aid in conflict settings presents significant challenges and frequently calls for flexible practices. However, as our investigators demonstrate and their work, flexibility cannot eclipse rigor.

Madam Chairman, Ranking Member Deutch, this concludes my prepared statement. I would be happy to take any questions that you may have.

[The prepared statement of Ms. Calvaresi Barr follows:]

Before the Committee on Foreign Affairs
Subcommittee on the Middle East and North Africa
United States House of Representatives

For Release on Delivery
Expected at
2 p.m. EDT
Thursday
July 14, 2016

Fraud Investigations Expose Weaknesses in Syria Humanitarian Aid Programs

Statement of
The Honorable Ann Calvaresi Barr
Inspector General
U.S. Agency for International Development

Chairman Ros-Lehtinen, Ranking Member Deutch, and Members of the Subcommittee:

Thank you for inviting me to this important hearing to discuss our ongoing efforts to ensure resources intended for the Syrian people are not wasted and reach those in need. As you know, our Government's financial commitment to provide humanitarian support in response to the Syria crisis exceeds $5 billion. Despite this major investment, instabilities in the region create challenges for the U.S. Agency for International Development (USAID), and the agency relies on implementing partners to get goods and services to where they are needed most. While implementers can be critical to carrying out USAID's mission, such arrangements require rigorous oversight to address risks.

My statement today focuses on our investigative actions—some of which are ongoing—to uncover and address fraud and waste, and the actions taken to date to stop identified abuse.[1] I will also highlight several program management concerns exposed by our investigations.

SUMMARY

Since February 2015, we have received 116 complaints of alleged abuse of USAID funds related to the Syria response, and have opened 25 cases to investigate these allegations. The most common fraud schemes identified to date involve collusion between vendors and implementers' procurement and logistics staff who accepted bribes or kickbacks in exchange for contract steering. We also identified a number of schemes involving product substitution of food and non-food items, inflated billing, and false claims. The Office of Inspector General's (OIG) investigations prompted USAID action that has resulted in more than $11.5 million in savings, 6 program suspensions, the removal of 10 employees of USAID implementers, and suspension or debarment actions against 15 individuals or companies involved in collusive bidding schemes.

Our investigative work has raised serious concerns about implementers' systems and USAID's oversight of assistance efforts that increased the program's vulnerability to exploitation. Given the urgency to deliver aid to in-need populations in Syria, for example, some of USAID's implementers used less than full and open competition to carry out large-scale procurements of food and non-food items. Concerns about implementers' responses to fraud allegations and their logistics, quality control, and monitoring procedures, as well as USAID's approach to oversight of these implementers have also emerged from our investigative work.

BACKGROUND

The March 2011 opposition against the Syrian Government escalated to an unrelenting civil war in the months and years that followed. This conflict has had significant humanitarian consequences that now extend beyond Syria's borders. Now 5 years into the conflict, millions have been displaced within Syria, and millions more have fled the country. The scale and duration of the crisis in Syria has put an unprecedented demand for humanitarian assistance in the region. According to the United Nations, people in Syria in need of food, water, shelter, health care, and

---

[1] To protect the integrity of its investigations and the welfare of the entities involved, OIG cannot discuss certain information regarding its investigative efforts.

other services increased from 2.5 million to 13.5 million between 2012 and April 2016. Approximately half of those in need have been internally displaced, and over half a million Syrians reside in areas under siege. Millions lack access to adequate drinking water and sanitation, and affordable foodstuffs are in short supply. The costs of certain commodities in Syria have soared, and the price of basic foodstuffs like bread has increased significantly. The conflict has driven up prices for other key goods and medical supplies and resulted in severely damaged infrastructure.

Since fiscal year 2012, USAID's offices of U.S. Foreign Disaster Assistance (OFDA) and Food for Peace (FFP) have coordinated and implemented humanitarian response activities.[2] OFDA and FFP work through implementing partners to procure and distribute non-food items, pharmaceuticals, medical consumables, bulk flour, food packages, and other relief to those in need in Syria. FFP works through implementers to provide food assistance to displaced persons in Syria and to refugees in Turkey, Jordan, Lebanon, Egypt, and Iraq.[3]

In fiscal years 2015 and 2016, USAID obligated more than $1.1 billion to fund humanitarian assistance for those affected by the Syria crisis, and OFDA and FFP report that they disbursed more than $835 million over this period (see Table 1).

Table 1. Cumulative Fiscal Year 2015 and 2016 U.S. Government Humanitarian Assistance Funding for the Syria Complex Crisis, as of March 31, 2016 (Dollars in Millions)

Office	Obligated	Disbursed
FFP	$814.9	$814.0
OFDA	310.1	21.8
Total	**$1,125.0**	**$835.8**

Note: Disbursement figures include disbursements of funds obligated prior to fiscal year 2015.

Source: USAID, response to Lead Inspector General request for information, April 19, 2016.

At the end of March 2016, OFDA and FFP had active awards with a combined total of 29 implementers. Implementers are responsible for ensuring that procured items are acceptable in

---

[2] The Department of State's Bureau of Population, Refugees, and Migration (PRM) also supports U.S. Government-funded humanitarian assistance activities. PRM works with partners to assist refugees, internally displaced persons, and conflict victims associated with the complex crisis in Syria.

[3] The scope of USAID activities in Syria extends beyond humanitarian assistance. In addition to humanitarian assistance, USAID's Office of Transition Initiatives supports efforts to provide basic public services such as waste and rubble removal (including unexploded ordnance), infrastructure rehabilitation, ambulances, and water tankers. USAID's Middle East Bureau provides support to restore essential services, including water, electricity, sewage systems, public use buildings, agricultural infrastructure, and market access.

terms of quality and quantity and are delivered in a timely manner, and that costs passed on to USAID are fair and reasonable. USAID headquarters staff and Disaster Assistance Response Team (DART) members deployed to Jordan and Turkey are, in turn, responsible for ensuring implementers carry out their responsibilities and that the programs and activities it funds address the most pressing needs in Syria and surrounding countries.

Continually changing security conditions create unique challenges for USAID and implementers to monitor and assess humanitarian efforts. USAID reported that U.S. Government personnel, including OFDA and FFP representatives, are not allowed in Syria. Although USAID staff can freely move within Turkey and Jordan to monitor activities, additional security approvals are needed when traveling to border areas near Syria. Ongoing conflict among combatants and shifting frontlines of engagement further complicate aid efforts. By the end of March 2016, 4.6 million people were living in besieged and other hard-to-reach areas.

USAID OIG provides independent oversight of humanitarian assistance operations in the region. Oversight of humanitarian and other U.S. Government activities and programs related to the Syria complex crisis are coordinated through the Lead Inspector General framework established under the Inspector General Act for oversight of overseas contingency operations.[4] This oversight framework was triggered in 2014 by the designation of Operation Inherent Resolve (OIR) as the U.S. Government's overseas contingency operation to counter the Islamic State of Iraq and the Levant (ISIL). Under this arrangement, the OIGs for the U.S. Departments of Defense and State, and USAID provide coordinated oversight and reporting. The OIGs work together to develop and execute a joint strategic plan for oversight of the contingency operation and to submit to Congress regular reports on the progress of OIR and corresponding oversight activities.

OIG INVESTIGATIONS UNCOVERED FRAUD SCHEMES, PROMPTING USAID ACTION

After the U.S. Government designated the response to the crisis in Syria a contingency operation, we ramped up our outreach to help ensure implementers identified and responded to fraud. Since January 2015, OIG special agents and investigators[5] have provided fraud awareness briefings to over 450 USAID and implementer staff responding to the complex crisis in the region. Based on our work in the field, we developed and issued *Fraud Prevention and Compliance*, a handbook that addresses internal control deficiencies, fraud indicators, fraud reporting requirements, and other protocols for avoiding or addressing abuse of program funds.[6] In addition, we informed our OIG counterparts at the Department of State of fraud schemes that could impact their department's

---

[4] This oversight framework is reflected in Section 8L of the Inspector General Act of 1978, as amended. An overseas contingency operation is a Secretary of Defense-designated operation in which members of the armed forces may become involved in military actions, operations, or hostilities against an enemy of the United States or against an opposing military force; or an operation resulting in the activation of members of the uniformed services during a war or national emergency declared by the President or Congress.

[5] In addition to U.S. direct hire criminal investigator special agents, USAID OIG employs Foreign Service National investigators who are locally employed at our offices around the world to support ongoing investigations and provide fraud awareness briefings.

[6] USAID Office of Inspector General, *Fraud Prevention and Compliance*, second edition, June 1, 2016.

operations and have been working closely with other donors and public international organizations[7] that could be affected by the same corrupt practices. To help protect international donor funds, our Office of Investigations proactively established the Syria Investigations Work Group in late 2015. The group consists of oversight organizations of other bilateral donors, such as the United Kingdom and Australia, as well as public international organizations. The group meets regularly to share information about ongoing investigations and investigative issues.

Since February 2015, we have received 116 allegations of procurement fraud, theft, and bribery, among others (see Table 2)—a significant increase in the total number of complaints made the year prior to that time.[8] Roughly two-thirds of the complaints OIG received relate to fraud and theft, but almost one-fifth involve diversions to terrorist groups. Most of the cases we opened relate to fraud. In total, we have opened 25 investigations related to nine implementers. To date, these investigations have prompted USAID to suspend vendors and other individuals or take other corrective actions against implementers that have committed procurement infractions.

Table 2. OIG Syria Complex Crisis-Related Allegation Types, February 2015 to June 2016

Allegation	Complaints	Cases
Fraud	35	21
Theft	40	0
Diversions to designated terrorist organizations[a]	21	1
Bribery or kickbacks	4	3
Other	16	0
Total	**116**	**25**

[a] The Department of Treasury's Office of Foreign Assets Control (OFAC) has designated ISIL and Jabhat al-Nusrah, a regional al-Qaeda affiliate, as terrorist organizations in Syria.

Since we began tracking USAID-reported losses in February 2015, we have recorded more than $1.3 million in quantified losses in flour, other food items, and non-food items, such as cash, medical equipment, pharmaceuticals, and winter kits. While some of these losses are documented as a result of fires, bombings, shelling, and airstrikes, many are reported as the result of petty theft and diversions. Some of the losses relate to diversions to OFAC-designated terrorist organizations.

---

[7] Public international organizations are organizations that perform international functions, are accorded the status of an international organization within the United Nations or by the country in which it is headquartered, and are not dependent on or controlled by any particular country. The World Food Program and International Organization for Migration are examples of public international organizations.

[8] OIG maintains a dashboard of its investigative developments related to humanitarian assistance in Syria. The dashboard is on OIG's web site, https://oig.usaid.gov/.

For example, when ISIL took control of Palmyra, Syria, a USAID implementer reported having to abandon 4,000 parcels of rations in its warehouse. Reports of ISIL diversions have declined; we received no reports of ISIL diversions in 2016, compared to 13 in 2015. Conversely, reports of Jabhat al-Nusrah diversions have increased from three in 2015 to five so far this year.

Fraud also poses a significant threat to assistance programs. Our special agents and investigators identified several types of schemes to defraud USAID out of program funds:

- **Collusion:** Our investigations in Turkey identified a network of implementer staff colluding with vendors who provide food and non-food items for Syria cross-border programming. Procurement staff accepted vendor bribes or kickbacks to provide competitive bidding data or manipulate the bid evaluation process, giving vendors an unfair advantage.

- **Product Substitution:** Our investigations in Turkey, Jordan, and Syria identified vendors that provided items of a lower quality or quantity than represented in the award. For example, one Turkish vendor delivered food ration kits with salt substituted for lentils. Had the fraud not been identified, the financial loss could have exceeded the $106,000 already incurred by the implementer. We also determined that non-food item kits in a warehouse in Syria that were awaiting delivery were missing items or included substandard products, such as tarps too small to fully shelter one adult and poor quality frying pans.

- **False Claims:** Our investigations of programs inside Syria revealed that implementers or their sub-awardees had billed USAID for services and goods that were not delivered or were delivered to ineligible or phantom beneficiaries. In one case, a Jordanian implementer operating under a sub-award fabricated documentation that it distributed non-food item kits to numerous communities in southern Syria when, in fact, the goods were distributed by another organization at its expense. Our investigation into this matter resulted in the termination of the sub-award and a total savings of $10.5 million.

Since June 2015, OIG has made seven referrals to Agency officials outlining internal control deficiencies and potentially illegal acts committed by implementer staff and commercial vendors. To date, the Agency has taken multiple actions in response (see Table 3). These measures have had a large-scale effect on the Syria assistance program. For example, in December 2015, USAID imposed programmatic suspensions on activities under six Syrian humanitarian response awards valued at $305.8 million. Eight months later, these program suspensions remain in place for awards valued at $239 million. With investigations ongoing, there is the potential for further referrals, show cause letters, employee terminations, and vendor suspensions and debarments.

Table 3. Agency Action in Response to USAID OIG Investigations

Agency Action	Purpose of Action	Number
Program suspension	To immediately halt activities of existing programs.	6
Show cause letter[a]	To formally request and obtain additional information to determine whether an organization is presently responsible or should be excluded from future contracting or assistance agreements awarded by the U.S. Government.	2
Suspension[a]	To temporarily exclude vendors and individuals from conducting business with the U.S. Government while they are under investigation or pending a legal proceeding.	14
Debarment[a]	To exclude vendors and individuals who have committed illegal acts such as embezzlement, theft, bribery, or making false statements from conducting business with the U.S. Government for a specified period of time.	1
Special award condition	To add special oversight conditions to the award that require the implementer to introduce improved internal controls before it can resume operations.	1
Employee termination	To remove employees of implementing partners for cause.	10
Partial program termination	To halt certain program activities because of deficiencies.	1

[a] Action taken by the Agency's Suspension and Debarment Official

INVESTIGATIONS RAISE CONCERNS ABOUT SYRIA ASSISTANCE PROGRAM CONTROLS AND OVERSIGHT

Our investigations raise a number of concerns about implementer practices for managing large-scale projects, as well as USAID's oversight of the humanitarian assistance program. These concerns have begun to inform our audit planning, which will include a strategy for drilling down on these issues to determine whether systemic management vulnerabilities exist and what additional actions USAID can take to ensure appropriate use of assistance funds.

Our investigations raise questions about the appropriateness of implementers' procurement policies and practices given the high-risk environment. For example, we identified:

- The extended use of emergency waivers to bypass established procurement policies and procedures—including full and open competition—in an effort to expedite procurements.

- A failure on the part of one implementer to conduct historical market analyses to detect inflated billing.

Our investigations also raise questions about implementers' logistics, quality control, and monitoring procedures. Our investigation of one implementer revealed a range of issues, including allowing vendors to ship items directly across the border without inspecting them in advance. In other cases, implementer staff accepted inappropriate clothing, substandard products, and other humanitarian items that did not meet invoiced technical specifications, including mattresses, blankets, and shelters. One implementer accepted kits based solely on their weight, not on their contents, thereby enabling a vendor's substitution of a less expensive food for a more expensive one to go undetected.

In addition, our investigations raise questions about implementer tracking of information and response to allegations of fraud. Some implementers did not pursue allegations or did not notify USAID or OIG of internal investigations into allegations of bid rigging, inflated billing, conflicts of interest, and other fraud. They also had evidence that corroborated the fraud allegations—including subject matter expert statements, emails, and company profile information—but concluded there was no evidence of fraud. For allegations we were informed of, we could not always obtain the information needed to assess allegations due to missing records, conflicting data protection laws, and other barriers to access.

Our investigations have also raised concerns about OFDA's oversight of implementers. DART teams did not include permanent subject matter experts to ensure procured items met the appropriate standards. OFDA generally did not require implementers to obtain prior agency approval of large subcontracts or establish requirements to inspect items before distribution to beneficiaries. However, in one case, OFDA is taking these steps in response to our investigative findings.

In addition to taking specific actions against firms and individuals that have committed fraud, USAID retained a third-party monitoring contractor to visit partner program sites and provide information to the Agency on the findings of those visits. According to OFDA, USAID plans to hire a compliance officer for its programs in Syria to promote financial and procurement integrity. OFDA and FFP are also working with our office to fund cost-incurred audits of five of the top six implementers in the region to determine whether costs billed to the U.S. Government were allowable and properly supported.

CONCLUSION

Providing aid in war-ravaged regions frequently calls for flexible contracting, award, and hiring practices to expedite the delivery of goods and services to the most vulnerable populations. However, as our investigations demonstrate, flexibility cannot eclipse rigor. Lax internal controls, monitoring, and oversight put taxpayer dollars at risk and, in the case of Syria, have delayed the delivery of millions of dollars of assistance to those in need. To address the concerns that our investigations have highlighted, we plan to advance audit work aimed at identifying and eliminating programmatic vulnerabilities before they can be further exploited. In the meantime, we remain committed to continuing our aggressive investigative work to address and mitigate related fraud, waste, and abuse.

Madam Chairman, Ranking Member Deutch, this concludes my prepared statement. I am happy to answer any questions you may have at this time.

Ms. ROS-LEHTINEN. Thank you. Thank you very much.

Really, thank you both for your testimony. There is certainly a lot to think about there, and I want to make sure that we thank you both and your teams for all the work they have done on this issue, for continuing to seek ways to help our agencies improve our oversight and the implementation of our assistance programs.

And, Dr. Melito, I will start some questions with you, if I might.

Tell us about why it is important for individuals and organizations operating in Syria to conduct a risk assessment? And if you could tell us how the U.N. internal control framework compares to ours. What are the—how do the requirements differ?

Mr. MELITO. Very good. A risk assessment is a jargony phrase that is pretty obvious. It is management, basically, trying to understand the challenges that their employees are having in the field. In this case, it is generally a procurement and logistics exercise where they need to understand which particular place they are using for buying things, storing things, moving things. And in the environment of Syria, there are a lot of complicating factors and a lot of heavy risks.

So risk assessment would really be a diagnostic on looking at what exactly is the situation on the ground, what are they facing, and then recognizing that some of this is very risky and then mitigating that by trying to make sure that there are oversight controls and just a good situational awareness on the part of management. That is why risk assessments are essential.

In terms of the internal control framework of the U.N., it is very similar. They are using international auditing standards which mirror, in a lot of ways, the ones that the U.S. Government uses. So when we have dialogues with them, we are pretty much on the same page. They are required to do risk assessments like the U.S. Government is. So there was no mismatch in discussions with them. They have the same requirements in that area.

Ms. ROS-LEHTINEN. Well, thank you. And all programs, and just about anything we do, are going to have at least some loss as a result of waste, fraud, abuse, diversion. It is sad to say, but it is reality based. Did either State or USAID provide you with a number on how much they believe is being lost to waste, fraud, abuse, or diversion? And do you get a sense from the agencies that they expect a certain amount to be lost as the cost of doing business in that they may have a formal or informal percentage they believe is acceptable?

Mr. MELITO. So GAO's perspective on this, and this is the auditing community as well, is that you need reasonable assurance. Now, reasonable assurance is something which has to be sort of understood at the corporate level, and they need to really think about where their particular tolerance is. But we are not talking about absolute assurance. I just want to drive that home. Because absolute assurance would be too expensive and it probably would prevent the humanitarian mission from going forward.

In terms of the magnitude of the losses, I do not think USAID or State have really any inkling on that. I don't think they have done the work to address that, nor have they thought about what is their risk tolerance. So I think that is a dialogue that they need to have moving forward.

Ms. ROS-LEHTINEN. Thank you.

And, Inspector General, I know you can't really go into details about the individuals and the entities, because in a lot of these cases, we are discussing ongoing investigations. But I did want to ask you a few questions about how that works when USAID says, okay, this implementing partner or this program is problematic, we need to cut ties. Because the vast majority of our assistance to—for Syria, for the humanitarian crisis, does go through the U.N., and obviously, there will be some overlap on the implementing partners and partner organizations. So when USAID suspends these individuals, these entities, these programs, they are no longer eligible to receive any U.S. Government awards, correct?

Ms. CALVARESI BARR. Yes, for a period of time.

Ms. ROS-LEHTINEN. And do we share this information with the U.N. or other organizations and implementing partners? And if so, what actions do they take or what actions do we expect them to take?

Ms. CALVARESI BARR. Let me make a few comments with regard to your question. First of all, I am very proud of the work that our office of special agents and investigations have done in this crisis.

When the overseas contingency operation was activated in 2014, proactive efforts went into the region, identified all of the implementers that were in that region, conducted 32 fraud awareness briefings with, you know, over 400 individuals, including USAID, DART teams, implementers, public international organizations. From that, these allegations have come forward, we opened cases and we found fraud.

USAID's response to that has been very, very promising. And what I will say to that is that we have ongoing communications with the various bureaus affected by this, whether it be OFDA, whether it be Food for Peace, regarding what we found. And they have taken actions in terms of suspensions, debarments, special conditions put on awards, employee terminations, and they have done so oftentimes without having a full record of our investigation.

And just to make a point of that, it is very difficult to sit down with organizations or with employees and say, you are being suspended, or you are being terminated, without the full underpinnings of an investigation. So this speaks to what USAID proper has done in response to that, and they have taken approximately 35 actions as a result of our work.

With regard to the U.N.—with regard to the U.N., what happens is—and as you noted in your statement, so much of the money flows through U.N. organizations, these, you know, PIOs, as we refer to them. It is absolutely important, because we do not have independent oversight of those operations, that information is shared.

Our office of investigations put together—and I know you asked me about this when we met the other day, and I am proud of it, so if I may hold it up for all of you—a fraud prevention and compliance handbook just for the region that goes out to everyone. This includes our U.N. counterparts. It includes all of the NGOs. It tells them what to look for. Our Syria Investigations Work Group, which we stood up, is a venue to actually brief the U.N.—our U.N. partners with its World Food Programme, on the fraud we are seeing. We share vendors lists where we have had issues, and we put, I would say, not only them on notice but pressure to say, you are likely working with the same implementers, now here, have at it. So you get the pressure points applied from a number of different perspectives, and I just wanted to take that moment because I am very, very proud of our——

Ms. ROS-LEHTINEN. I am glad that you did. Because I can foresee an instance where maybe these guys are defrauding the U.N. or other implementing partners as well or perhaps even the U.N. continues to work with them after we provide these agencies with our information.

And just to finish up with the U.N., perhaps I will ask this of both of you, how does working through the impact, the U.N. impact our ability to exercise the kind of oversight that we would require if we were working with implementing partners directly in terms of things like transparency and accountability? How does that change?

Mr. MELITO. So we do have audit authority over the implementing parties. We do not have audit authority over the U.N. That said——

Ms. ROS-LEHTINEN. Could you say that again?

Mr. MELITO. So—here we go. I said we do have audit authority over implementing partners, but we do not have audit authority over U.N. agencies. That said, I have done, over the last 10 years, a series of reports involving U.N. agencies where I have generally gotten excellent cooperation. And I think that is in recognition of how important the U.S. is as a donor, and I think they would want to cooperate with the U.S. Government. So I can't point out a case where I wasn't ultimately able to get the information that GAO needed to do its work. So while it is an indirect process, ultimately, I think it's been a successful process.

Ms. CALVARESI BARR. I would just add to that, again, to underscore our Syrian Investigations Working Group. We also have reached out sort of on a one-to-one basis. I just recently met with the World Food Programme Inspector General. I know that he was in town working with folks in the bureau as well, and the pressure is really being applied saying, you are going to be working with these same implementers, with these same vendors. We are relying on you to provide this aid.

And I think it is also important to point out the very important role that the U.N. plays. They provide these bulk items in terms of humanitarian assistance into the region. They can have staff in Syria. You know, we need them. They provide a huge role and help us achieve this mission.

We just need to stay on top of them, make sure that the right oversight, the monitoring, the internal controls are established, and that USAID puts some pressure on them to do it.

I will tell you, you can be assured, we will be on it.

Ms. ROS-LEHTINEN. I understand that.

Congratulations to both of you for the great work that you do. It is important to carry that message to the U.S. taxpayer. Thank you.

And with that, my good friend, the ranking member, Mr. Deutch.

Mr. DEUTCH. Thank you, Madam Chairman. And I also want to express my personal gratitude and our committee's—subcommittee's gratitude for the work you have done here. I think it is really important.

Ms. Barr, I would like to pick up where the chairman left off, on what happens when there is a suspension for fraud activities?

I would tell my friend, if he would like to wait, I will sit in as the chair. It is not something that I get to do. I am just kidding.

Ms. ROS-LEHTINEN. No problem.

Mr. WEBER. Will the gentleman yield the rest of his time?

Mr. DEUTCH. If I get to be chairman, I will.

When there is a program that is suspended, there is a quick—how quickly can we move to find a partner to pick up whatever support that program was providing, and how do we ensure that, for all of the really necessary oversight efforts that you both have been so deeply engaged in, that we don't wind up with serious gaps in providing the lifesaving services that are so important?

Ms. CALVARESI BARR. I can tell you that USAID works very, very promptly to try to identify other implementers that we—the aids—that the aid can resume to get to those in need, and they work very heartily and swiftly at that. There sometimes is a delay. I am not going to say there isn't a gap in that aid going out, because it certainly does happen, but these companies needed to be suspended. As our results show, you know, we have six suspensions currently out in place, and those are six program suspensions that fall under some major, major implementers.

The best thing that we can do, and I think it is in line with Tom's statement and the work of GAO overall. USAID's role is really to establish a baseline set of internal controls, procurement practices that they are going to require for any implementer, regardless of who they are. You know how many are out there. The range of their—the rigor and their controls is going to be vast. There should be a baseline standard set for what those internal controls should be, what those good procurement practices should be, and those should be monitored from USAID.

And given that we don't have the oversight authority with the U.N., you know, establishing those expectations, setting them, making that a condition of the money flowing to those in need is—it sounds quite simple, but it hasn't been uniformly applied. And I think it speaks to the recommendations that the GAO report made and certainly to the observations that are coming out of the outcomes we have found.

Mr. DEUTCH. I appreciate that. It is a really good suggestion.

Dr. Melito, I wanted to acknowledge, I think, what we have all already been discussing. In the conflict zone like Syria, we can't have U.S. personnel on the ground. So we rely on remote monitoring and management.

The report discusses many of the challenges of remote management, but if you could just elaborate on these challenges, and in this particular environment, why it is different in terms of what agencies and implementers have dealt with previously. Why is it such a concern for oversight in particular?

Mr. MELITO. So as you mentioned, U.S. Government officials cannot enter——

Mr. DEUTCH. Yes.

Mr. MELITO [continuing]. Syria. So for a normal humanitarian assistance effort, you would expect on-the-ground monitoring by U.S. Government officials. They would be looking at the warehouses, they would be watching the beneficiaries receive their assistance, making sure it is up to the quality and quantity that we paid for.

In this case, the information they have to rely on is coming from people who are inside the country telling them subsequently what has happened. That is indirect. Now, they trust a number of these parties correctly, but it is still, though, something which is indirect for them.

So what they do, they end up trying to triangulate, trying to get information from multiple sources. They are trying to use some new technologies such as geotagging pictures of things, and that is all very good, but it will never be as effective as being able to see it yourself. So that in itself means the risk of fraud and diversion is greater. Because of the indirectness of the monitoring, you are in a situation and environment which heightens the risks, and that needs to be recognized and addressed.

Mr. DEUTCH. And can you, just in the remaining time that I have, can you try to put a face on this? When—we are obviously concerned. We are grateful for the report, and we are concerned about instances of bribery and bid rigging and failure to provide the material that had been committed to or contracted to provide.

But what does that actually mean for the people who were to have been on the receiving end? And it is—we know what the impact is on our taxpayers, and that is why this is so important, but just how awful is it to the people on the ground who are in such desperate need?

Mr. MELITO. So in your statement and in the chairman's statement, talk about the magnitude of it, 13½ million people inside the country. The U.S. Government estimates it is reaching about 4 million. So that is—the U.S. Government is doing great. It is the single largest donor, but it is only reaching a subset. Any diversion from that is even lower than that.

So from our perspective, this is literally taking food out of the mouths of babies. I mean, it is taking resources that are in desperate need and not putting it where it needs to be and, instead, in hands of people who you are not designating as a target. So it has a direct humanitarian impact. It is not just that this is a bad deed that we—you don't have them for criminal reasons. It is hurting the humanitarian mission, and that needs to be kept front and center.

Mr. DEUTCH. I am—I appreciate that.

And just, Ms. Barr, I would say to you, again, as grateful as we are for the focus on the impact, dollars are one thing and they are important. And as watchdogs, it is important that you focus on that. But the work that you do is so terribly important, because the proposals that you made, if they are followed, will mean not only that taxpayers can be satisfied that their tax dollars are being used the way they are supposed to, but that those tax dollars are actually being used to save lives. And we are grateful for that.

I yield back. Thanks, Mr. Chairman.

Mr. WEBER [presiding]. Mr. DeSantis, if you are ready, if you are in a hurry, I will yield to you for 5 minutes.

Mr. DESANTIS. Well, thank you, Mr. Chairman.

And thanks to the witnesses.

So, obviously, we appreciate you looking into this. We know there is going to be a certain amount of waste, fraud, and abuse, unfortunately, when you have operations going on in this area. But did you get the approximate numbers on how much U.S. assistance inside Syria may have been lost due to waste or fraud?

Mr. MELITO. GAO does not have a number. That would be the kind of number that AID would need to produce itself. I would defer to my colleague if she has any information.

Ms. CALVARESI BARR. What I can tell you is what we reported and what we know, is $1.3 million in losses. And those would be losses that are due to fires, bombings, parachutes not opening when pilots drop, but they also refer to diversions to other terrorist organizations.

Mr. DESANTIS. What about fraud?

Ms. CALVARESI BARR. And with regard to fraud, sometimes things, they are stolen, but in terms of fraud, it is hard to quantify the total dollar on fraud.

Mr. DESANTIS. I think you have to view it differently. I mean, if you are in a hot zone and you have aid that is intercepted by terrorists, that is much different than if the money is just being frittered away. And so I think it is important for us to know the distinctions on there.

Let me ask you this, Mr. Melito. There have been a number of attacks on medical facilities and humanitarian workers in Syria. Did either USAID or State provide a list of all instances in which one of the belligerents in Syria attacked any of our partners delivering aid or seized any of our assistance?

Mr. MELITO. So in our report, we talk about some U.N. information on that. So U.N. reports about 89 humanitarian workers have been killed since the conflict has started, and there have been hundreds of attacks on medical facilities and also attacks on food deliveries and such. And then the U.S. in my report, we also talk about when the city of Palmyra fell, food that was stored there fell into the hands of ISIS.

Mr. DESANTIS. So do you have an estimate on the numbers and the costs in terms of the assistance that has been implicated by any of those? I guess State didn't give you any information?

Mr. MELITO. We are unaware of either agency doing a comprehensive assessment of that.

Mr. DESANTIS. Okay. There are U.N. Security Council resolutions in place for accessing movement for humanitarian assistance inside Syria, but from your report, it seems that Assad's regime may be in violation of these resolutions. So how many requests do you know has the regime denied since the beginning of 2015?

Mr. MELITO. The U.N.'s reporting that they are only receiving about—approvals about 20 percent of the time. I think the number that we report is 110 requests and 13 approvals. So in—what is going on there, it pays to talk a little bit about it.

So when the U.N. wishes to go outside of these Assad-controlled areas, to the areas outside of our control, they need permission for what the items are; they need permission to travel on the roads; they need permission to cross checkpoints; they need visas for employees to come in, and they have not been getting the approvals 90 percent of the time. And when they do get it, they say that it is very slow and uncertain.

Mr. DESANTIS. So even if they are not actually denying it, they are basically undermining it with the process. And so how have State and USAID responded to those limitations?

Mr. MELITO. Well, the U.S. is part of the international community's effort to broaden the delivery of services. So there was two Security Council resolutions that passed in 2014 and 2015, which made it legal for delivery of services across the border. And that is what most of the international NGOs are doing. They are delivering assistance from Turkey and Jordan mostly, and that is against the wishes of the regime. So there, they are saying that the humanitarian assistance is more important than the wishes of the regime.

This that we are referring to as denials is areas that are still within the control of the regime or at the border of the control of the regime. So it is two different ways of delivering services.

Mr. DESANTIS. The agencies that concurred with your recommendations, how long do they have to implement these and for you to close the recommendations?

Mr. MELITO. GAO tracks its recommendations for 4 years. But generally, agencies respond within 1 or 2 years. And given the importance of this issue, I am hopeful they will do it quickly.

Mr. DESANTIS. Well, I thank you. I thank the witnesses.

And I yield back.

Mr. WEBER. I thank the gentleman.

The gentlelady from Florida is recognized.

Ms. FRANKEL. Thank you, Mr. Chair.

Thanks to the witnesses.

I want to start by saying that I think most of us agree that what is going on in Syria is one of the greatest humanitarian tragedies of our lifetime since World War II. And there is no question that we have to do whatever is reasonably possible to be part of efforts to relieve some of the suffering, the starvation, the homelessness. And because we are going to lose a generation of people, of young people who are not getting health care or getting education. So I want to say that I appreciate your efforts to try to make sure that it is done right.

My first question is, in your review of these—of the programs, can you tell us, are any programs doing better than others? And what is it that—where things are working, what makes it different?

Ms. CALVARESI BARR. I think it goes back to what we said in terms of what is missing. And what is missing is when there aren't clear expectations regarding what should be internal control processes and good procurement practices that need to be in place, given the fact that you are in these highly unstable and stable environments, the fact that it is remote monitoring and remote oversight. Those kinds of things call for special conditions, and I think it is incumbent upon USAID—it all starts with them, setting those baselines of standards, holding its implementers, NGOs to that standard, the U.N. organizations to that standard, and make sure that the reporting does come back. There has to be that basic minimum set of circumstances and requirements put in place, and currently, that is missing.

Ms. FRANKEL. In your review, were you able to determine where aid is actually getting through to? Because I know there is—you have regime-held areas and you have ISIL-held areas and then you have, I guess, other areas.

Mr. MELITO. So the U.S. agencies, both State and AID, pay very close attention to the map, basically. And it divides up, generally, to areas that are controlled by the Assad regime and the areas right near that, which includes a lot of the seized areas and hard-to-reach areas. And the other part is the areas near the borders of Turkey and Jordan.

They have different implementing partners for those two, so the U.N. is able to operate within the Assad-controlled areas of the country. The international NGOs cannot operate there, but they can operate across border. And in all those cases, State and AID pay very close attention to groups which are not permitted to receive assistance. And we've got very good assurance that there is no assistance going currently to ISIS-controlled areas.

That all said, it is a very fluid situation on the ground and a very complicated situation on the ground that has to be constantly monitored, but those are the kinds of things that the agencies are balancing.

Ms. FRANKEL. So is aid going to the Assad-controlled areas?

Mr. MELITO. Yes. The U.N. is—there are a number of individuals in the Assad-controlled areas which are in desperate need. So the U.N. is providing assistance there, but it also is deploying out of those areas into the besieged and hard-to-reach areas. That said, it is not reaching nearly as many of those people as it wishes to. That is the reference to being denied access by the regime.

Ms. FRANKEL. So Assad is not—which countries are being used, which borders, to get the assistance across?

Mr. MELITO. So it is predominantly Turkey in the north and Jordan in the south. Those are the two main.

Ms. FRANKEL. And how cooperative have their governments been and their military that is on the border?

Mr. MELITO. That is probably appropriate for both the State and AID, but my understanding is they have been getting good cooperation.

Ms. FRANKEL. That they have been given good cooperation. All right.

I have nothing further. Thank you.

I yield back.

Mr. WEBER. All right. Thank you.

I am sorry, Dr. Melito, did you just say that the Turkey and the Jordan military have not been very cooperative?

Mr. MELITO. I said have been cooperative.

Mr. WEBER. They have been cooperative.

Mr. MELITO. That is also a question for USAID.

Mr. WEBER. Okay. I don't think your button is on.

Mr. MELITO. Yes. Have been. Sorry.

Mr. WEBER. Have been. Okay.

Mr. MELITO. I want to be clear on that.

Mr. WEBER. All right. Very good.

A lot of questions. Is it Calvaresi Barr?

Ms. CALVARESI BARR. Calvaresi Barr.

Mr. WEBER. Calvaresi Barr?

Ms. CALVARESI BARR. Calvaresi Barr.

Mr. WEBER. Calvaresi Barr. Okay.

Ms. CALVARESI BARR. Very good.

Mr. WEBER. I can do this.

You said earlier, I think, that there were nine partners that had been either used or identified as bad players. Refresh my memory on that.

Ms. CALVARESI BARR. We have seven referrals that we have given to USAID, and they involve nine implementers.

Mr. WEBER. Implementers.

Ms. CALVARESI BARR. Implementers, right. And the program suspensions that we have in place are six. And, again, I just want to underscore, this isn't a wholesale suspension of the implementers at large. These are programs within these implementer——

Mr. WEBER. In what period of time? Is that the last year?

Ms. CALVARESI BARR. This is data pretty much coming from 2014 through the present.

Mr. WEBER. So the last not quite 2——

Ms. CALVARESI BARR. Since the overseas contingency operation.

Mr. WEBER. I got you. And when aid is delivered, do you have evidence that it was delivered?

Ms. CALVARESI BARR. So I think part of the challenge definitely lies in that. And I think we are calling for recommendations along the lines of the types of reporting back you might require under some of these basic standards that you set.

Could it be a phone call? Could it be a printed receipt? Are there ways to put more branding or tags or labeling on the food, on the nonfood items to come back? But because we are in this kind of remote business and we are reliant on others, we have to come up with creative mechanisms to determine that, in fact, that aid did reach those it was intended for. Currently, again, that is a mixed bag, but I think if there are reporting standards and other kind of baselines to establish it, it could help.

Mr. WEBER. Well, they can put chips in animals, right, that can be tracked? So if you put one on just every 50th, you know, item or so?

Ms. CALVARESI BARR. Yes.

Mr. WEBER. Has that been looked at?

Ms. CALVARESI BARR. It is something that, I think, is under consideration, talking about a whole range of options. But it all starts with even checking at the warehouses before it crosses the border, whether it be in Turkey, in Jordan. You know, it starts there, and then what happens in transit, because, again, this is remote monitoring. This is remote oversight.

Mr. WEBER. So if you lose an implementer, do you have a ready supply of people lined up on the list that are applying to be implementers?

Ms. CALVARESI BARR. I represent the oversight community, so not being the USAID proper or others to know exactly what their full list of contingents are, I know that for the aid going into Syria, they are working with approximately 29 implementers now. But oftentimes, when these situations occur, folks go into the region very, very quickly in order to deliver the aid, to deliver the assistance, and that—you know, that creates some vulnerabilities in and of itself. They are new to it. We are relying on them. It creates a perfect storm for what our investigations have found.

Mr. WEBER. It makes me wonder if there is not a preferred implementer that actually—this is probably not the right term—but gets a kickback or is a favorite. They get a pass, they get to come on deep into Syria with the least amount of hassle. Has that been your findings or no? Are there preferred implementers, one does a better job than the other?

Ms. CALVARESI BARR. You know, hard to say if there are preferred, but I can tell you that all of the implementers have to show themselves as presently responsible. And when that doesn't occur— and there are certain criteria for that—that is when program suspensions and other things happen.

So there are some implementers out there that have very, very good, as I said in the beginning, tight controls, good internal— know what internal controls are brought into play.

Mr. WEBER. So that they all get treated—I guess I am asking, are they bipartisan, is what I am asking? They all get treated the same.

Ms. CALVARESI BARR. They all get treated the same.

Mr. WEBER. Okay. Good. And has there ever been an instance where there is a recovery of any aid? Aid gets lost, gets taken, and once that happens, it is done.

Ms. CALVARESI BARR. Our work, one of the impacts that we talked about is the fact that we brought in $11.5 million in savings as a result of our fraud investigations. And what that means is when we uncovered the fact, like in the case of a Jordanian NGO that was to provide assistance and had another NGO actually do the transport and deliver the items but yet charged USAID for it when it was incurred by another NGO, shut down that program, shut down that operation. That one in and of itself was $10.5 million of the $11.5 million. So——

Mr. WEBER. Were there criminal charges that ensued in that instance?

Ms. CALVARESI BARR. In some cases—these are ongoing investigations. There could be criminal implications as a result of it, but I can tell you it resulted in a number of employee and implementer terminations, suspensions, debarments.

Mr. WEBER. Okay. And then, Dr. Melito, I think you said some aid workers were killed, and I didn't quite hear what you said. Did you say eight or nine or 89?

Dr. MELITO. According to the U.N., 89.

Mr. WEBER. Eighty-nine. Okay. Okay. And then furthermore, Turkey and Jordan were the two areas that the aid came out of, but did you say that they really didn't—that the Assad regime really doesn't prefer that?

Dr. MELITO. So until these Security Council resolutions were passed, it wasn't clear that they could do that, because it would be violating the sovereignty of the country. Normally, you have to basically get the permission of the country to provide assistance.

Yes, the Assad regime is not supporting the cross-border assistance and they are doing it against his wishes, but it is an international—it is legal now because of the Security Council resolutions.

Mr. WEBER. So is it because Turkey and Jordan signed onto the resolution?

Dr. MELITO. The Security Council resolutions have the force of law internationally. So they gave permission for that kind of assistance to occur.

Mr. WEBER. So would Assad rather they come from Russia, from Iran, from Iraq? Where would he rather they come from?

Dr. MELITO. He would rather it was in his areas of control.

Mr. WEBER. His areas of control, so he can parlay out the goods——

Dr. MELITO. He can determine when and how, yes.

Mr. WEBER [continuing]. However he wants to. Well, that makes sense, I guess, if you are Assad.

Okay. And then finally, your office hasn't yet conducted audits of USAID programs in Syria. Is that right?

Ms. CALVARESI BARR. We, in fact, have done some audits in the recent past. There are about three audits that were done in the 2014 timeframe. With that said, they were very specific audits looking like a survey of OFDA activities. There were audits regarding Office of Transition Initiatives work there, Food for Peace work.

One thing, if I could take a moment, just since I have been sworn in into this position as the new IG at USAID, one thing that we need to do better—and I am working very quickly to do so—is to make sure that our work informs at the policy and the strategic level and goes after the highest risk areas. We have done tremendous work on Food for Peace programs over the years. They are very, very program transactional specific, but it doesn't raise oftentimes to the higher level.

As a result of our investigative work, a number of program concerns and questions have been raised now regarding internal controls, procurement practices. We are now focusing our audit work and our audit plans going forward on those very real effects that our Office of Investigations have found.

So we have some work to do in that area. And I don't want to belittle what USAID IG has done before, but we need to link it to those policy-level decisions and the bigger picture and the highest risk and crosscutting work across the board, and I am committed to do that.

Mr. WEBER. Well, that is encouraging to hear. So you will have a plan put together and we will see you back next week?

Ms. CALVARESI BARR. Can I have an extra week on top of that?

Mr. WEBER. All right. Well, my time has expired. I am going to yield back.

Ted, any more questions?

Mr. DEUTCH. No.

Mr. WEBER. All right. This hearing is concluded. Thank you very much.

[Whereupon, at 3:20 p.m., the committee was adjourned.]

APPENDIX

MATERIAL SUBMITTED FOR THE RECORD

SUBCOMMITTEE HEARING NOTICE
COMMITTEE ON FOREIGN AFFAIRS
U.S. HOUSE OF REPRESENTATIVES
WASHINGTON, DC 20515-6128

Subcommittee on the Middle East and North Africa
Ileana Ros-Lehtinen (R-FL), Chairman

July 7, 2016

TO: MEMBERS OF THE COMMITTEE ON FOREIGN AFFAIRS

You are respectfully requested to attend an OPEN hearing of the Committee on Foreign Affairs, to be held by the Subcommittee on the Middle East and North Africa in Room 2172 of the Rayburn House Office Building (and available live on the Committee website at http://www.ForeignAffairs.house.gov):

DATE: Thursday, July 14, 2016

TIME: 2:00 p.m.

SUBJECT: U.S. Humanitarian Assistance to Syria: Minimizing Risks and
                   Improving Oversight

WITNESSES: Mr. Thomas Melito
                   Director
                   International Affairs and Trade
                   Government Accountability Office

                   The Honorable Ann Calvaresi Barr
                   Inspector General
                   Office of the Inspector General
                   United States Agency for International Development

By Direction of the Chairman

COMMITTEE ON FOREIGN AFFAIRS

MINUTES OF SUBCOMMITTEE ON _____ *the Middle East and North Africa* _____ HEARING

Day__ *Thursday* __Date___ *July 14, 2016* ___Room_____ *2172* _____

Starting Time ___ *2:19 p.m.* ___Ending Time ___ *3:20 p.m.* ___

Recesses |____| (____to ____) (____to ____) (____to ____) (____to ____) (____to ____) (____to ____)

Presiding Member(s)

Chairman Ros-Lehtinen, Rep. Weber

Check all of the following that apply:

Open Session ☑   Electronically Recorded (taped) ☑
Executive (closed) Session ☐   Stenographic Record ☑
Televised ☑

TITLE OF HEARING:

U.S. Humanitarian Assistance to Syria: Minimizing Risks and Improving Oversight

SUBCOMMITTEE MEMBERS PRESENT:

Chairman Ros-Lehtinen, Reps. Chabot, Weber, DeSantis, and Zeldin
Ranking Member Deutch, Rep. Frankel

NON-SUBCOMMITTEE MEMBERS PRESENT: *(Mark with an * if they are not members of full committee.)*

HEARING WITNESSES: Same as meeting notice attached? Yes ☑ No ☐
(If "no", please list below and include title, agency, department, or organization.)

STATEMENTS FOR THE RECORD: *(List any statements submitted for the record.)*

TIME SCHEDULED TO RECONVENE _____
or
TIME ADJOURNED ___ *3:20 p.m.* ___

_____
Subcommittee Staff Director